THE DISAPPEARING FORESTS

UNDERSTANDING GLOBAL ISSUES

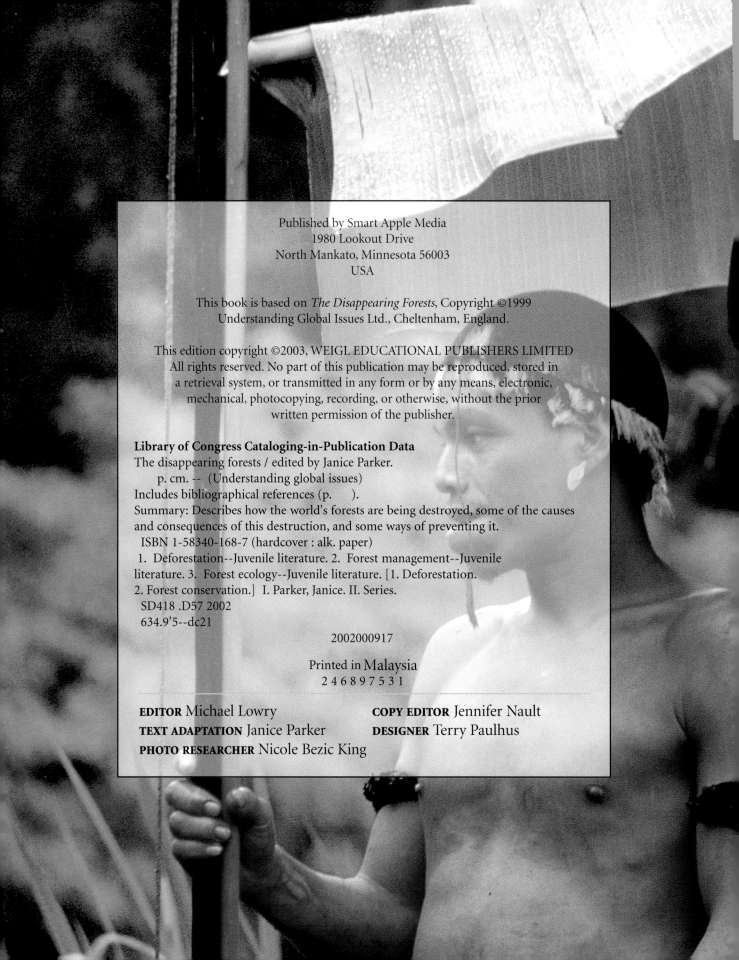

Published by Smart Apple Media
1980 Lookout Drive
North Mankato, Minnesota 56003
USA

This book is based on *The Disappearing Forests*, Copyright ©1999
Understanding Global Issues Ltd., Cheltenham, England.

Library of Congress Cataloging-in-Publication Data
The disappearing forests / edited by Janice Parker.
    p. cm. -- (Understanding global issues)
Includes bibliographical references (p.   ).
Summary: Describes how the world's forests are being destroyed, some of the causes
and consequences of this destruction, and some ways of preventing it.
  ISBN 1-58340-168-7 (hardcover : alk. paper)
 1. Deforestation--Juvenile literature. 2. Forest management--Juvenile
literature. 3. Forest ecology--Juvenile literature. [1. Deforestation.
2. Forest conservation.] I. Parker, Janice. II. Series.
 SD418 .D57 2002
 634.9'5--dc21

                                2002000917

                        Printed in Malaysia
                        2 4 6 8 9 7 5 3 1

EDITOR Michael Lowry   **COPY EDITOR** Jennifer Nault
TEXT ADAPTATION Janice Parker   **DESIGNER** Terry Paulhus
PHOTO RESEARCHER Nicole Bezic King

Contents

Introduction

Trees are very important to our planet. They act like Earth's lungs and help control the climate around the globe. Trees also protect soil from **erosion** and provide habitats for a wide variety of plants and animals. Forested regions are also home to millions of aboriginal people who rely on the forests for food and shelter. Cutting down vast numbers of trees not only affects the people, plants, and animals that live in those forests, but also the rest of the world.

For more than 30 years, **environmentalists** have been drawing attention to the large amount of forest cover that is cut down or destroyed each year. A major loss of forest cover in a concentrated area is called deforestation. Although warnings about the harmful effects of deforestation have increased, the practice still continues, especially in the poorer countries known as the developing world. Since 1980, forest coverage in the developing world has decreased by more than 772,000 square miles (2 million sq km)—an area three times the size of the state of Texas.

The world's remaining rainforests may disappear by 2030 if deforestation continues at current rates.

There are many reasons for deforestation. These reasons include a demand for forest products, the settlement of forested land, and political corruption. In many regions of the world, cutting down timber is also seen as a quick way to make money. In parts of Africa and Asia, money made

> *For more than 30 years, environmentalists have been drawing attention to the large amount of forest cover that is cut down or destroyed each year.*

from illegal logging is used to finance the military. Worldwide, the demand for paper pulp, which is made from wood, has doubled since 1975, and continues to grow.

Until the late 1980s, most large forests were government owned. Publicly owned land is usually managed for the long-term good of the nation. Such was the case in the former Soviet Union and in many developing countries, where old-growth forests were left largely undisturbed. With the spread of **capitalism**, many publicly owned forests were sold to private companies and individuals. Privately owned

forests are often considered to be an easily exploitable resource. As a result, they are managed for profit and not for conservation.

While many governments in the developed world now have strict standards concerning deforestation in place, many countries in the developing world do not. This often means that rich countries protect their own forests while they deplete those of poorer countries. Europe, North America, and Asia have a huge demand for wood and the untouched forests of Russia and the developing world have been too tempting for logging companies to ignore.

There is no simple solution to deforestation. One idea is debt-for-nature swaps, where developed countries agree to erase the debt of developing countries if those countries agree to protect their forest reserves. Another solution is chain-of-custody certification, which ensures that the timber used in wood products comes from sustainably managed forests. Any potential solution must consider the relationship between the developed and developing worlds. Without drastic action, the majority of natural old-growth forests will soon be lost forever, along with the wildlife and native cultures that inhabit them.

The Importance of Trees

ost developed countries cut down their old-growth forests many years ago. However, since 1980, there has been an increase in overall forest cover in developed countries, partly as a result of replanting. But this increase is misleading because the quality of forest cover has decreased. The secondary-growth forests that have replaced the old-growth forests lack the biodiversity of the original forests. Other forested areas have been turned into **plantations**, which specialize in growing

---

In some areas, the trees have been severely damaged by pollution.

---

just one type of tree. In other forested areas of the developed world, the trees have been severely damaged by pollution.

In the developing world, pollution damage may be less severe than in the developed world, but forests are continuing to vanish at an alarming rate. This trend is very serious because the **tropical** forests, located mainly in developing countries, provide habitat not only for millions of people, but also for a large proportion of

the plant and animal species in the world.

Trees are important for a variety of reasons. These include:

Climate Control

Trees act like the lungs of the planet. Trees take in carbon dioxide and release oxygen into the air. This makes the planet's air breathable. Trees also play a major role in the water cycle. They absorb water from the earth through their roots and leaves, returning the moisture into the air through a process called **transpiration**. Transpiration is the mechanism by which trees and other plants release water through their leaves. The water is released in the form of vapor, which then gathers as clouds in the sky.

A substantial loss of trees in an area creates a break in the water cycle and can cause drought. Cherrapunji, a town in northeast India, was once listed in encyclopedias as the wettest place on Earth. Recently, deforestation has changed the climate of the region, making it drier. These changes have created severe water shortages for the people living in Cherrapunji.

Prevention of Soil Erosion

Forests play an important role

▨ **Deforestation is a major cause of soil erosion. The Food and Agriculture Organization (FAO) estimates that erosion accounts for the loss of between 18,800 and 26,600 square miles (50,000–70,000 sq km) of farmland worldwide each year.**

▨ **Increasingly, large areas of forested land are being turned into plantations, such as this sugarcane plantation in Colombia, to support the global demand for food.**

in protecting the land from soil erosion. Tree roots help bind soil so that it is less likely to be carried away by water or wind. Soil erosion occurs when there is nothing to prevent soil, in particular **topsoil**, from being washed away by rainwater and rivers or blown away by wind. Trees also help to slow down the movement of water and wind through a region. For

example, a forest is much better at preventing a flood from spreading than a grass-covered field.

Erosion and soil loss over large areas around the world threaten the planet's ability to produce food. More than 22 billion tons (20 billion t) of topsoil are lost each year. Much of it is washed into the oceans. The mud and soil enters rivers, lakes, and oceans, damaging the ecosystems of fish and other aquatic animals and plants. Studies in Malaysia have shown that the amount of mud and soil in rivers was between 40 and 150 times higher in logged areas than in undisturbed forests. Soil erosion can also lead to flooding, since there is less earth to absorb water.

Protection of Species

Forests, in particular tropical forests, are an important source of genetic diversity. Between 50 and 90 percent of all species of plants and animals that live on land are found in forests. As forests disappear, so do many plants and animals that may have medicinal or nutritional value for humans. The specialized knowledge that **indigenous** peoples have of local plants and animals is also being lost, as native populations are forced to move from their traditional lands.

BIOMES AND ECOSYSTEMS

A biome is a geographical region on Earth that contains a distinctive community of living things. There are seven biomes: tundra, taiga, **temperate** forest, tropical rainforests, desert, grassland, and ocean. The tropical rainforest is the richest source of life on Earth. More types of plants and animals live in tropical rainforests than anywhere else on the planet. Tropical rainforests are mostly found around the Equator. Temperate forests cover large parts of the Northern Hemisphere. These forests are mainly deciduous, which means the trees lose their leaves in winter.

Each biome is made up of different ecosystems. An ecosystem is a community of plants, animals, and nonliving components, such as soil, nutrients, and water, which coexist within a larger biome.

Temperate forests can be found in the United States, Canada, Europe, Russia, China, and Japan.

 British Columbia, in western Canada, is renowned for its old-growth rainforests, many of which are under threat from logging companies.

KEY CONCEPTS

Old-growth forests Old-growth forests are made up of trees that are often very large and very old—sometimes hundreds of years old. They contain at least two different species of trees, trees of many different ages and sizes, a **tree canopy** made up of several layers, standing dead trees, and fallen logs. Certain types of plants and animals can only be found in old-growth habitats. Primary forests, original forests, and natural forests are other terms for old-growth forests.

Secondary-growth forests
Secondary-growth forests are forests that have been replanted or have regrown naturally. Trees in secondary-growth forests are usually younger and smaller than those found in old-growth forests. Secondary-growth forests often contain fewer types of trees. Fewer types of animals, plants, and fungi live in secondary-growth forests than in old-growth forests.

Developing countries
Sometimes collectively referred to as the Third World, developing countries are those whose economies and industries are still developing. Developing countries are generally very poor and rely on aid and assistance from developed countries.

Developed countries
Developed countries are those that have strong economies and sophisticated industries. Developed countries are also called industrialized countries.

Deforestation Deforestation is the cutting down of forests for forest products, or to clear land for agriculture, construction, or other human activities. Many international organizations use more specific definitions of deforestation.

Biodiversity Biodiversity is the biological diversity, or number of different species of plants and animals, in a given habitat. Untouched tropical forests are the richest regions of biodiversity in the world. It is estimated that 80 percent of the world's species remain undiscovered.

Counting the Trees

In 2000, the United Nations' Food and Agriculture Organization (FAO) estimated that the world's forests covered about 30 percent of the land area of the planet. About half of all forest cover is made up of tropical or **sub-tropical** trees. The other half is made up of temperate or northern species. Most forest cover is natural. While the number and size of planted forests are increasing, they still make up only about three percent of global forest cover. Large areas of untouched natural forest account for about 40 percent of global forest cover. Deforestation

---

Different organizations often come up with very different statistics on forest cover.

---

threatens the remaining 57 percent of the world's untouched natural forests.

Many organizations collect statistics on the world's forests, including the FAO and the World Conservation Monitoring Center. The information collected by these groups helps scientists develop strategies to manage the world's forests. Different organizations often come up with very different statistics on forest cover and forest loss. This is because each organization defines "forest" in different ways. The World Conservation Union (IUCN) lists 25 different types of forests, whereas the FAO regards forests as either "open" or "closed." An "open forest" is one in which the tree canopy covers between 10 and 40 percent of an area. A "closed forest" is one in which the tree canopy covers more than 40 percent of an area.

Global forest cover can be estimated in two ways. One method involves gathering statistics from each country. The other method uses satellite images of Earth's surface. Neither method is perfect. With each method, there are still disagreements on the definition of forest cover. Different organizations also use different definitions.

Images taken by satellites, such as *Landsat 7*, provide vital information about Earth's surface, including forest cover.

RONDÔNIA, BRAZIL (1975)

6 mi

Images from the United States Geological Survey taken over time by *Landsat* satellites illustrate the advance of deforestation in parts of the Amazonian rainforest of Rondônia, Brazil. The red areas indicate healthy vegetation, while deforested and urban land appears as light blue. In 1975, the majority of the land is forested. The light blue line on the right side of the image is a road.

RONDÔNIA, BRAZIL (1986)

6 mi

In 1986, a satellite image of the same region illustrates how deforestation begins along roads and then fans out to create a "feather" or "fish bone" pattern. Between 1978 and 1988, the estimated average deforestation rate in Brazil was 6,000 square miles (15,000 sq km) per year.

RONDÔNIA, BRAZIL (1992)

6 mi

By 1992, the feather patterns have become more pronounced, as deforestation consumes the region.

The FAO defines deforestation as the loss of more than 90 percent of the tree canopy in a given area. This means that even if as much as 85 percent of the tree canopy has been removed, it is not classified as deforestation. The FAO's definition also does not take certain factors into account. These factors include the replacement of old-growth forest by secondary-growth forest, disease or pest infestation, the age of the trees, or tree plantations. The various statistics on global forest cover and deforestation are, at best, rough estimates.

Every 10 years, the FAO publishes a comprehensive report on the status of the world's forest resources. The most recent report was entitled *Global Forest Resources Assessment 2000* (*FRA 2000*).

Forest survey crews provide vital information about the state of the world's forests.

It is the most complete analysis of the world's forests to date. The publication contains statistics covering timber products as well as non-wood forest products. Along with considering economic factors, the report also examines forest health, biodiversity, and the ability of forests to remove carbon dioxide from the air. By studying the data provided in the *Global Forest Resources Assessment 2000* (*FRA 2000*) report, scientists are able to estimate future changes in forest cover.

Every two years, the FAO provides updated reports in their publication called *State of the World's Forests*.

MAPPING THE WORLD'S FORESTS

The World Conservation Monitoring Center (WCMC) has worked with the World Wildlife Fund (WWF) to produce a world map showing forest cover and protected areas. The map breaks forests down into five broad types—temperate needle leaf, temperate broadleaf, and mixed, tropical moist, tropical dry, and mangrove forests. Using the WCMC data, the World Resources Institute estimates that the planet was covered by about 23 million square miles (60 million sq km) of forest before the spread of human civilization about 8,000 years ago.

The Committee on Earth Observation Satellites (CEOS) has recently developed a project called the Global Observation of Forest Cover (GOFC). The aim of GOFC is to produce a current picture of world forest resources using satellite images and other data collected from governments. The organization hopes to complete its first report by 2002.

■ Taiga, also known as boreal forests, accounts for 33 percent of the world's total forests. Boreal forests are dominated by evergreen trees, such as pine, fir, and spruce.

State of the World's Forests reports on the status of forests, recent changes in policy, and other important issues that concern the forest industry. In 1990, for example, the FAO conducted a special survey of tropical forests. The information in this survey was collected using remote sensing techniques. The survey covered a small portion of the tropical forests of Latin America, Africa, and Asia. For 2000, the FAO included temperate and northern, or **boreal**, forests as well as tropical forests in its survey.

The FAO publications provide the best information about the world's forests. However, the FAO has had problems in gathering information from about 200 different governments. Some of these countries are not interested in forestry statistics and have not gathered new data in the past 10 to 20 years. Some countries have used imprecise tree-counting methods or have downplayed deforestation. This means that statistics gained from improved data-gathering techniques, such as remote sensing, may be surprising. Despite the problems in collecting statistics, scientists are certain that deforestation is widespread.

KEY CONCEPTS

Remote sensing Remote sensing is the gathering of information from a distance. Many techniques are used to collect remote sensing data, including radar, aerial photography, and satellite imagery. Remote sensing is particularly useful for gathering information on the environment.

FAO The FAO was founded in 1945 and is one of the largest agencies of the United Nations. The FAO is the lead agency for agriculture, fisheries, forestry, and rural development. The FAO, which has 183 member countries, works to eliminate world hunger, improve agricultural practices, and conserve natural resources.

USGS Created in 1879, the U.S. Geological Survey (USGS) is an independent government agency that researches and provides scientific information on natural resources and important environmental topics, such as forest cover and water quality.

Duties: The preservation of forests, including timber and ecosystem management
Education: A bachelor's degree in forestry
Interests: Working outdoors to protect nature

Navigate to the Society of American Foresters Web site: www.safnet.org for information on related careers. Also click on www.environmentaljobs.com for more information on careers in forestry.

Careers in Focus

Early in their careers, foresters divide their time between working in the field collecting data and working in the office, or laboratory, analyzing data. When outdoors, the forester performs a variety of tasks, including tree measuring, land surveying, water testing, tree planting, and forest fire fighting. Foresters are generally in excellent physical shape, since the outdoor work can be difficult and strenuous. Foresters work outdoors in all sorts of weather, from intense heat to freezing blizzards. They also travel great distances, often walking through dense vegetation and over unknown terrain. Foresters also need excellent communication skills, as they interact with loggers, landowners, environmental groups, and the general public.

There are three different types of foresters—the industrial forester, the consulting forester, and the government forester. The industrial forester typically works for a person or a company in the private sector, such as a logging company. The industrial forester is often hired to purchase forests from landowners. They must first take an inventory of the forested area and make an appraisal of the forest's worth. If the land is purchased, the forester will then oversee the logging of the trees to make sure it meets the requirements of the logging company and the government's environmental regulations.

The consulting forester works with landowners, often performing many of the same duties as the industrial forester. A consulting forester will appraise a forest for a landowner so that they may negotiate with logging companies. Consulting foresters also help landowners manage their forests. They oversee operations, such as tree planting and pesticide application.

The government forester manages forests owned by the government, such as state parks and national forests. In addition to forest management and protection, government foresters design campgrounds and recreational areas.

Forests Teeming with Life

One of the most serious issues of deforestation is the loss of habitat for thousands of species of plants and animals, leading to the extinction of these species. This loss of biodiversity can have a drastic effect on the population of other species, including humans. The human species depends on only a small percentage of the world's plants and animals for survival. These include the species used as food, medicine, and shelter. Scientists know very little about the other millions of species. As the world becomes increasingly industrialized, the number of different plant and animal species is being greatly reduced. If the species that humans depend on disappear, there may be no new species left to replace

them. As more plants and animals disappear, scientists also lose the chance to study new species that could help cure certain diseases or famine.

The biodiversity of tropical rainforests is especially high. A single acre of rainforest can contain more species of plants, insects, birds, reptiles, and mammals than a whole country in the industrialized world. Yet between 1970 and 1985, more than 76,600 square miles (200,000 sq km) of rainforest were cut down or destroyed in Brazil alone. As a result, large numbers of plants and animals have likely become extinct. Other countries have also cut down large areas of forest, leaving only isolated areas that are too small to provide adequate habitat for many species of plants and animals. Small, protected areas of forests cannot make up for the loss of large natural forests. Most of the large remaining areas of untouched forests are in the Amazon basin in South America, the Congo basin of central Africa, and Siberia in northern Russia.

The developed world relies on certain major food crops, such as wheat, rice, maize, soybeans, and potatoes. Only a few crops from tropical regions, such as bananas, coconuts, coffee, and sugarcane, are used in the industrialized world. Even though tropical forests contain a large number of different edible plants, fruits, and nuts, very few are consumed in the industrialized world. Large food companies can make more money by growing a limited amount of crops that are easy to produce. This means that many types of plants, fruits, and nuts that are less profitable to grow and sell are ignored. For example, while there are many

▨ **Deforestation threatens the habitat of jaguars, which are found in the rainforests of Central America and Brazil.**

SUSTAINABLE FORESTS

Consumer pressure is forcing the big forest companies in the developed world to use sustainable forest management practices. Sustainable forests are logged in a way that has the least possible impact on an ecosystem. When a forest is properly managed, it can continue to support many different types of plants and animals. If enough trees, especially older trees, are left standing, a forest can sustain a healthy ecosystem.

The International Tropical Timber Organization (ITTO) was founded in 1983. The headquarters for the ITTO are in Yokohama, Japan. Members of the ITTO gather to discuss issues related to tropical forests. The aim of the organization is to set up guidelines on the export or import of tropical timber products that come from sustainably managed forests. Most of the trees that are cut down in tropical forests, however, are not exported. They are used as fuel for cooking, heating, and in local industry. Deforestation in tropical areas will continue as long as the population continues to grow and no alternative cheap fuels are made available.

types of apples, only a few are grown and sold in grocery stores.

Similarly, only a limited amount of forest products are available to consumers. The developed world uses only a few of the thousands of types of trees in the world's rainforests. These include hardwoods, such as mahogany and ebony, and trees that produce consumer goods, such as coconuts, bananas, cocoa, or latex for rubber. There are many other tree species of which the industrialized world has little knowledge.

The forests of developed countries have far fewer species of plants and animals than those in tropical zones. One reason for this lack of biodiversity is the climatic differences between the two regions. Another reason is the replacement of old-growth forests with secondary-growth forests. Secondary-growth forests have usually been replanted by humans and contain only one species of tree. These forests, or plantations, are like "tree deserts," because few birds, insects, or mammals live in them. Europe has only a few of its original forests left. These forests, such as Kailua in Finland and Rimakabbo and Jelka in Sweden, give scientists an idea

Logging roads open the way for large-scale deforestation by providing access to miners, farmers, and other users.

of what temperate forests were once like. They may also provide a blueprint for the restoration of European forests.

Thick forests once covered Scotland. The region was as rich in birds and mammals as the untouched forests of Canada or Russia. The original Caledonian Forest in Scotland, which was made up of trees, such as birch, oak, and aspen, is gone. Today, most tree cover in the region is needle leaf, such as spruce and fir, in secondary-growth forests. The loss of tree species in Scotland was very gradual. Similar losses of biodiversity have occurred in the United States, the Mediterranean region of southern Europe, the Middle East, and China.

Today, the most serious forest losses are taking place in Asia and Latin America. Deforestation is also occurring in Africa, where poverty has driven millions of people to cut down trees to use as firewood or to create farmland. Tropical forests cover less than seven percent of the African continent.

KEY CONCEPTS

Hardwoods Hardwood lumber is made from broadleaf deciduous trees. Deciduous trees lose their leaves in the fall. Hardwood lumber is an excellent building material and is used to make baseball bats, musical instruments, and wood flooring. Trees classified as hardwoods include aspen, beech, birch, maple, and oak. There are also tropical hardwoods, such as ebony, mahogany, and rosewood. Tropical hardwoods are used in fine furniture.

However, these forests are home to more than half of Africa's plants and animals. About 15,400 square miles (40,000 sq km) of forests in Africa alone are being destroyed each year.

Deforestation also exposes wildlife to dangers such as hunting. Many animal species are over-hunted and in danger of extinction. Roads built by logging companies make it easier for hunters and poachers to move into previously untouched wilderness areas. With improved access to wildlife, the sale of "bush meat" has increased dramatically. Bush meat is the meat of animals, such as

---

Deforestation also exposes wildlife to dangers such as hunting.

---

monkeys, chimpanzees, gorillas, elephants, and leopards. Bush meat is sold in markets around the world as an exotic delicacy.

It is also popular in poor communities that cannot afford other foods. In some countries in Africa, bush meat is close to 75 percent cheaper than farmed meat, such as cows. People around the world are also willing to buy rainforest products such as reptile skins, bird feathers, orchids, and exotic pets. Many people use animal products such as tiger bones, rhino horn, and bear bile as traditional medicines.

A QUESTION OF HARMONY

People who move to rainforest areas usually clear plots of land on which to live and farm. Indigenous groups, on the other hand, are often thought to live in harmony with nature. Unfortunately, this is not always true. Most human societies have taken part in the abuse and overuse of natural resources. Some examples of indigenous groups destroying trees are the deforesters of Easter Island and the forest-burning aborigines in Australia. The size of a group's population has a great effect on the harm they cause to the environment—the larger the population, the greater the pressure on the land. However, many indigenous groups live in harmony

in the rainforests. The mixed economy of the Yanomami peoples in Brazil, and the tree gardens of the Chagga peoples on the slopes of Mount Kilimanjaro in Tanzania, are two such examples. The Yanomami lived in harmony with the rainforests until forest fires and mining companies destroyed much of their land. The Chagga plant a wide variety of trees and plants that support one another and the environment. However, sustainable rainforest living is not possible if a population outgrows its resources. Once a population grows too large, the forest can no longer recover from human activity and overuse.

Increasing pressure from the outside world means that the Yanomami's traditional way of life is under threat.

Duties: The study of plants, including cell structure, reproduction, and environmental influences
Education: A bachelor's degree in **botany**
Interests: Nature and biology

Navigate to the Environmental Careers Web site: www.eco.org for information on related careers. Also click on www.botany.org/bsa/careers for more information about botany jobs.

Careers in Focus

One of the most important roles of the botanist is to determine the effects of human activity, such as logging and pollution, on plant life. Plant life includes everything from microscopic fungi and algae to giant sequoia trees. Not only do plants provide the planet with oxygen, they are also a source of food for a large percentage of the world's animal species, including humans. Botanists who study the interactions of plants with their environment, and with other living organisms, are interested in ecology. Botanical research helps conservationists manage parks, forests, and other natural areas.

Another important role of the botanist is to discover and study new species of plants. This is especially important in the areas of the world where deforestation may destroy potentially valuable, yet undiscovered plant species. Undiscovered plants may contain the key to the cure for a disease or become the basis of a new food crop.

The field of botany is broad, and offers many areas of specialization, including genetics, biochemistry, plant breeding, and seed analysis. As well as forestry, botanists can also be found working in a variety of related fields, such as agriculture, **horticulture**, and soil science.

Products of the Forest

Timber is the main product of forests, but it is not the only one. Timber may not even be the forest product that makes the most money. The clear-cutting of trees for timber may be less profitable than a limited felling of trees and the gathering of forest products, such as fruits, nuts, and resins.

However, clear-cutting is widespread in countries that are becoming increasingly industrialized. During colonial times, India lost millions of trees to fill the demand for **railroad ties** in the 19th century. Forests in Europe and the tropics were cut down to supply **charcoal** for furnaces during the Industrial Revolution. Tropical hardwoods were also used to build furniture. Even earlier, in the 1700s, the demand for shipbuilding and housing used up European oaks. As cities grew, the surrounding forests were cut down for building materials and fuel. Today, coal and oil are used more often than wood for fuel

in the developing world. Still, forests are being cut down for building materials and for the pulp and paper industry, which is the world's largest consumer of wood.

The 1998 World Wildlife Fund (WWF) report, *Investing in Tomorrow's Forests*, found that about two-thirds of the world's forests are **commercial** forests. Though timber is often very profitable, it can be expensive to process and distribute. Many companies use methods that will make the most

---

The pulp and paper industry is the world's largest consumer of wood.

---

money, such as planting areas with only one species of a fast-growing tree.

Commercial forests that produce palm oil, rubber, coconuts, and bananas make up only a small part of the global forest cover. These plantations are often classified as agricultural land rather than forest. Companies plant fast-growing trees such as pine, **eucalyptus**, and acacia to supply pulp to the paper industry. If forest ecosystems are to be preserved, the commercial forest companies must adopt methods that

SHOPPING THE WOODS

The world's forests produce a wide variety of products. About half of roundwood production, which is the total log harvest from felled trees, is used for fuel. The other half is used in industries, such as those listed below.

CONSTRUCTION	timber, plywood, chipboard, hardboard, poles, posts, veneers
MANUFACTURING	cellulose, pulp for paper, rubber, textiles, plastics, wood tar
ADDITIVES	oils, dyes, **tannin**, chewing gum, ointments, perfumes, resins, adhesives
FOOD	nuts, fruits, flavoring extracts, syrups, oils
HEALTH	medicines
SOLVENTS	turpentine, pine oil
ENERGY	fuelwood, charcoal

▬▬ Natural rubber is made from the milky white juice of the rubber tree. Plantations in the Far East, India, Africa, and South America supply the world's natural rubber.

consider biodiversity as well as profitability.

Some of the world's largest companies are forest-product companies. Thousands of other companies are involved in logging or processing timber. Some pay little attention to environmental concerns. Large international timber companies look for areas to log all over the world. Some companies avoid strict laws in their own countries by cutting down forests in developing countries where the laws may be less strict. Most governments in the developed world require companies to provide details on all of their logging operations. Companies in the developing world, on

> *In the future, scientists may be able to create trees that will grow faster, resist disease, and contain less lignin.*

the other hand, do not have to follow such rules.

Unlike food crops, which have been genetically altered to produce higher yields, tree species have been left largely in their natural state. In the future, scientists may be able to create trees that will grow faster, resist disease, and contain less **lignin**. Trees with less lignin are more useful in pulp and paper production. The creation of genetically modified trees is likely to be the next step in the process of forest industrialization. Currently, companies are working to create trees that are more productive.

NON-WOOD FOREST PRODUCTS

Non-wood forest products (NWFP) are natural products, other than wood, that can be harvested from forests. NWFP play an important role in the developing world, where nearly 80 percent of the population relies on them for their health and nutritional needs. NWFP are also gaining popularity as alternative exports to lumber. Cleared rainforest land used to raise cattle is worth $60 per acre, and if timber is produced, the land is worth $400 per acre. If renewable resources are harvested, such as NWFP, the land is worth $2,400 per acre.

NWFP	WHAT IS IT?	WHAT IS IT USED FOR?	LOCATION
Henna	Leaf extract	Dye	North Africa, Asia
Brazil nuts	Nut	Food	South America
Maple syrup	Tree sap	Sweetener	North America
Cinnamon	Tree bark	Spice	India, East Africa
Ginseng	Herb root	Herbal medicine	China
Eucalyptus oil	Oil from leaves	Perfumes	Australia, China
Pyrethrum	Flower extract	Insecticides	Kenya
Gutta percha	Natural latex	Golf balls, teeth fillings	East Asia
Benzoin	Resin	Perfumes	Southeast Asia

While the modern paper mill is a complex industrial factory, the fundamental principles of paper making have remained unchanged since its invention in China in A.D. 105.

KEY CONCEPTS

Roundwood Roundwood are logs or other round pieces of wood cut from trees. These wood products are used in their natural form and include products such as firewood, posts, poles, and pulpwood.

Clear-cutting Clear-cutting is a logging technique in which all of the trees in an area are removed at once. By getting rid of old-growth forest, clear-cutting destroys animal habitats. It also reduces biodiversity in an area. Clear-cutting can also lead to soil erosion and leaves behind an unattractive landscape if new trees are not planted.

Industrial Revolution The Industrial Revolution refers to a time period when machines changed the way people worked and lived in many parts of the world. The Industrial Revolution began in Great Britain in the 1700s and spread throughout Europe and North America in the 1800s. The industrialization of manufacturing was the result of new technologies, such as power-driven machines, and new working methods, such as factory production.

Map of World Forest Loss

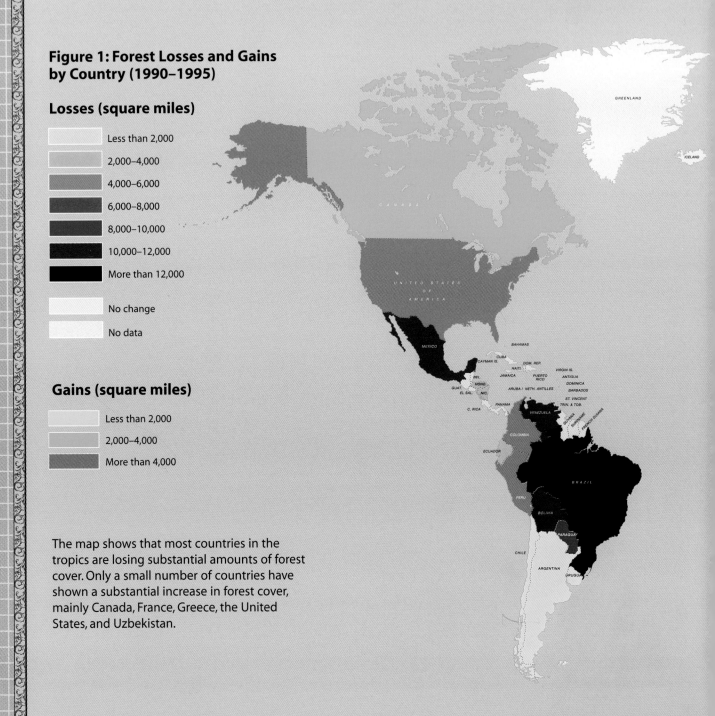

Figure 1: Forest Losses and Gains by Country (1990–1995)

Losses (square miles)

- Less than 2,000
- 2,000–4,000
- 4,000–6,000
- 6,000–8,000
- 8,000–10,000
- 10,000–12,000
- More than 12,000

- No change
- No data

Gains (square miles)

- Less than 2,000
- 2,000–4,000
- More than 4,000

The map shows that most countries in the tropics are losing substantial amounts of forest cover. Only a small number of countries have shown a substantial increase in forest cover, mainly Canada, France, Greece, the United States, and Uzbekistan.

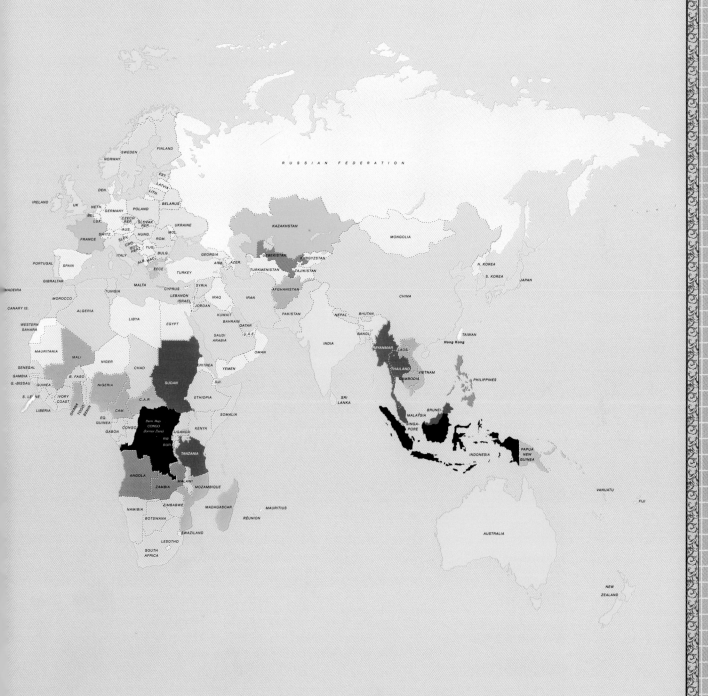

Source: FAO

Charting the World's Forests

Figure 2: Forest Plantation by Region (2000)
(Percentage of world's plantations)

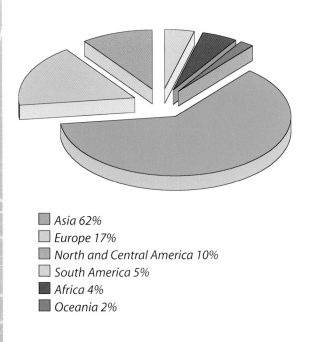

- ■ Asia 62%
- □ Europe 17%
- ■ North and Central America 10%
- □ South America 5%
- ■ Africa 4%
- ■ Oceania 2%

Figure 3: Distribution of Forest Cover (2000)
(Percentage of the world's total forest cover)

- Europe 27% □
- South America 23% □
- Africa 17% ■
- Asia 14% ■
- North and Central America 14% ■
- Oceania 5% ■

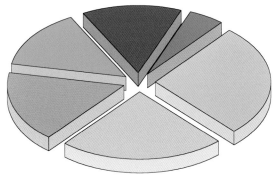

Figure 4: The Big Eight (2000)
Forested area (thousand square miles)

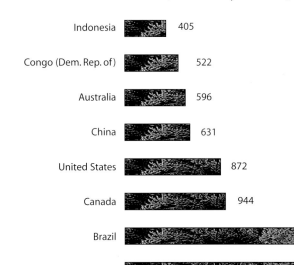

Indonesia	405
Congo (Dem. Rep. of)	522
Australia	596
China	631
United States	872
Canada	944
Brazil	2,100
Russia	3,300

Just 8 of the world's countries contain 63 percent of its forests. This puts a special responsibility on these nations. The preservation of tropical forests is of particular concern because of the biodiversity they harbor. Ten countries—Brazil, Indonesia, the Democratic Republic of Congo, Peru, India, Colombia, Bolivia, Sudan, Papua New Guinea, and Venezuela—account for about two-thirds of all the world's tropical forest. Brazil alone harbors one-third of all tropical rainforest.

Figure 5: How Wood is Used (1996)
(Forest product consumption)

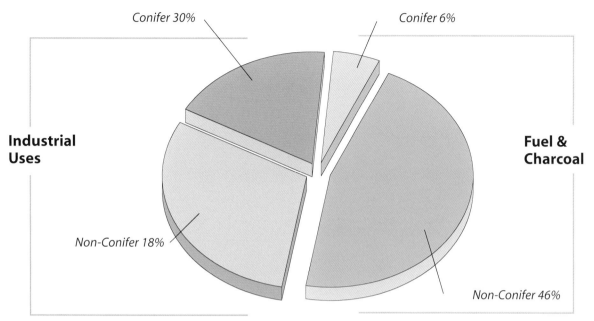

Conifer 30%

Conifer 6%

Industrial Uses

Fuel & Charcoal

Non-Conifer 18%

Non-Conifer 46%

Total Consumption 120 billion cubic feet (3.4 billion cu m)

In developed countries, wood is used mainly for industrial purposes, with pulp and paper products becoming ever more important. In the developing world, by contrast, some 80 percent of cut timber is used for fuel, either as firewood or charcoal.

Figure 6: Net Change in Forest Cover by Region (1990–2000)
(Net change in thousand square miles per year)

Africa is the biggest regional loser of forests in the world. Between 1990 and 2000, Africa lost more than 20,500 square miles of forest cover.

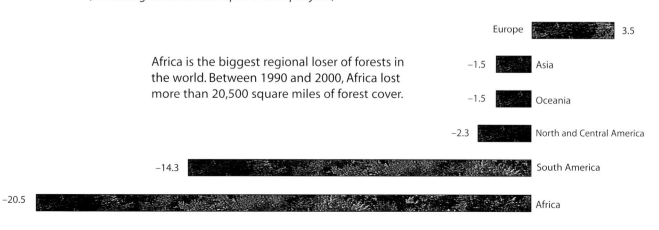

Europe 3.5

−1.5 Asia

−1.5 Oceania

−2.3 North and Central America

−14.3 South America

−20.5 Africa

The Loss of Forests

Although deforestation in developing countries has subsided, a forested area the size of Kansas is still being lost each year. The remaining tropical forests in Latin America, central Africa, and southeast Asia are all affected by forest loss. The old-growth forests in the United States, Canada, and Russia are also at risk.

While logging is not the only cause of deforestation, it opens up forests for other uses. Cutting through a forest to clear the way for a road or a pipeline interferes with wildlife. It also creates a route for other people, such as farmers, hunters, and land developers, to move into the area. Logging also increases the risk of forest fires. When a forest loses its leafy tree canopy, the sun penetrates to the forest floor, drying the vegetation and increasing flammability.

Forests once covered about 75 percent of China. Today, that number has fallen to 14 percent, despite China's ambitious tree-planting programs. Countries such as El Salvador, the Gambia, and Haiti have lost almost all of the forest cover they once had. Forest loss is causing environmental and climatic changes in these countries.

Forests once covered about 75 percent of China. Today, that number has fallen to 14 percent.

In the 1970s and 1980s, large areas of forest in Latin America were cut to clear land for cattle ranching. The meat from these ranches was often used in American fast-food restaurants. It is said that six square yards (5 sq m) of forest had to be cleared to make enough meat for one hamburger. Many of the big ranches quickly failed because the soil was not useful as pastureland for cattle. In the forest, nutrients are stored in the trees, and not in the soil. As a result, forest soils are not very fertile once the trees have been removed. Half of the ranches established on deforested land in the Amazon River basin never produced any beef at all and were abandoned.

In Brazil, the federal environment agency has tried to receive funding and political backing to help protect the nation's forests. The country has experienced problems enforcing forest conservation laws. Gold mining is destroying the tropical ecosystem in parts of the Amazon. Large-scale mining operations need to clear forest

Colombia's national tree is the endangered wax palm. It is threatened by deforestation and livestock, which eat the seedlings and prevent regrowth. The remaining trees are vulnerable to disease.

WHERE HAVE ALL THE FORESTS GONE?

In 2000, the global forest cover was about 14.9 million square miles (38.7 million sq km). Industrialized countries lost most of their forest cover before 1900, as they cut down trees to clear land for farming or to provide timber and fuel for economic development. The mixed forests of cedar, oak, beech, and pine that once covered parts of southern Europe were removed long ago by humans in search of wood for fuel and building materials. Woody shrubland now covers large areas of southern Europe that were once covered by trees. After Europeans settled in North America, the region experienced the worst period of deforestation in history. About 656,400 square miles (1.7 million sq km) of forest in the eastern United States was quickly reduced to about 38,600 square miles (100,000 sq km). Since 1950, the developing world has experienced similar levels of deforestation.

in order to access the gold. Mining operations also produce massive amounts of waste, which pollutes the water supply and kills the trees.

The enforcement of forest conservation laws is also a concern in Indonesia, parts of Africa, and Russia. In these areas, illegal logging has increased because of poverty

Wealthy countries have also cut down large amounts of old-growth forests.

and political instability. In mid-1999, hundreds of fires were set in Indonesia in order to clear large areas of land.

Even wealthy countries have cut down large amounts of old-growth forests. Canada is also guilty of deforestation. In 1993, for example, the government opened half of the magnificent coastal forests of Clayoquot Sound on Vancouver Island to commercial logging.

NATURE'S LOGGERS

Fire is nature's way of clearing a forest of waste, such as dead vegetation. Fire also helps prevent insect or fungi outbreaks. Certain types of trees even depend on fire to scatter their seeds. Throughout human history, fire has also been used as a way to transform the land. It was widely used by Native Americans and Australian Aborigines to clear land. Today, foresters try to prevent forest fires, even those started by natural causes. This leads to the buildup of large amounts of dead material in forests. Eventually, this dead material can lead to crown fires that create enormous amounts of heat and are very destructive. Crown fires are extremely dangerous fires that occur at the tops of trees. They are most often set off by human error or lightning.

Insects and diseases can also destroy forests. International trade has increased the risk of the spread of disease and insect infestations from other parts of the world. Trees, and other species, are more at risk from insects and diseases that come from other parts of the world than from local, well-established pests and diseases. This is because they have developed some resistance to local pests and diseases. Since biodiversity is one of the best protections against disease, plantations of single tree species are more likely to be devastated by diseases and pests. Examples of damaging insect pest outbreaks include gypsy moth infestations in European oak forests, plantation moths in Australia and the Philippines, and the Asian long-horned beetle in the United States.

KEY CONCEPTS

Illegal logging In many places in the world, particularly developing countries, illegal logging is a major cause of deforestation. Illegal logging is any logging performed by individuals or companies that does not follow the laws or forestry policies of the region.

Forest conservation laws Many countries have tried to create laws that will prevent the destruction of forests. Forest conservation laws are a start, but it is often very difficult for governments to make sure such laws are being followed.

Causes of Deforestation

There is rarely a single cause of deforestation. According to the United Nations' Food and Agriculture Organization (FAO), the main causes of deforestation are the increase in subsistence agriculture and the clearing of forests to create land for resettlement, agriculture, and the construction of roads, dams, and pipelines. Some environmentalists, however, believe that large, **multinational** logging companies are the major cause of forest destruction. In reality, the causes of deforestation vary according to local situations. In a 1991 report, the World Bank found that companies producing timber, banana, and cattle products were the main cause of deforestation in Costa Rica. Before this report was published, it was believed that the major cause of forest loss was large numbers of people clearing forests for settlement.

Poverty in the developing world is perhaps the biggest factor of all—and the hardest to fix. In Africa, local poverty is often blamed for loss of old-growth forest. But poverty is clearly not the cause of deforestation in places such as California or British Columbia.

One or more of the following factors are usually identified as the causes of deforestation:

Population pressure

There are three times as many people in the developing world living close to forests as there were in 1950. People cut down forests for firewood and to clear land for farming. These forests are being destroyed much faster than they can regrow.

Farming and resettlement are the primary causes of deforestation in Latin America.

Economic hardship

Poverty and unemployment, combined with population growth, contribute to deforestation. For millions of people, making use of forest resources is their only means of survival. These people are not in a position to consider the negative long-term effects of forest loss.

Foreign debt

In an effort to pay off foreign debt, many developing countries are producing **cash crops** for export. Examples include bananas in Central America and palm oil in Indonesia. These crops are often grown on poor-quality rainforest soil. The poor soils mean that larger areas of forest must be cleared in order to achieve adequate harvests.

Government policies

Some countries, such as Brazil and Indonesia, encourage people to move into forested areas. The

For millions of people, making use of forest resources is their only means of day-to-day survival.

new settlers often think that it is necessary to destroy the forest in order to turn it into what they consider to be productive land. The United States did the same

This aerial photograph shows a resettlement project and the resulting deforestation, in Bolivia. The light-colored areas are fields of soybeans.

with its own wilderness in the 19th century. The effects were not as serious in the U.S. because the soil was more fertile. However, in Brazil and Indonesia, the poor rainforest soils and high erosion rates result in unproductive land when forests are cleared.

Money-making potential

Trees are very profitable once they are cut down, so cutting down timber is a way to make money quickly. Most companies are concerned more with short-term profits than with long-term sustainability. The logging process is also very wasteful. In order to remove a large tree, loggers have to destroy many smaller surrounding trees, which are often connected by hanging vines. As one tree is cut down, it pulls down others connected to it. Often, 5 to 10 times more trees are destroyed than are used.

Improved access

Roads providing access into forests typically destroy 10 to 15 percent of the area being logged. This damage is then

With wood increasingly difficult to find, many rural families in developing countries must spend between one and five hours each day collecting it.

Slash-and-burn agriculture is when farmers deliberately set forest fires to clear land for crops or grazing. After a few years, the nutrients in the soil are used up and the farmers move to other plots of land that are cleared by fire. When practiced by individual families, slash-and-burn agriculture does not destroy large areas of land. However, when this method is used over larger areas for commercial crops, huge amounts of forest can be destroyed.

increased as road access brings in new settlers, hunters, miners, and traders. Large transportation routes, such as the Trans-Amazon Highway, have a much more serious effect on the environment than small roads.

Weak property rights

In places where no one owns the trees or only short-term logging contracts are granted, there is little incentive to conserve the forest. Logging companies want to remove trees as quickly as possible. In some regions, it is traditionally believed that everyone owns the land.

Environmental responsibility

The people cutting down the trees are generally not held

responsible for the long-term costs of deforestation, such as soil erosion and loss of biodiversity.

The need for fuel

The need for wood as fuel is especially important in the developing world. Most wood burning is done in traditional stone fireplaces that waste more than 90 percent of the heat energy. The use of charcoal is popular in cities because it is easy to transport, but charcoal is an extremely inefficient energy source.

Many people fear that in order to meet market demand, protected forests in North America will soon be opened to logging.

Market demand

Consumers in rich countries want tropical hardwoods for consumer products, such as furniture and musical instruments. More than 40 percent of all tropical timber imports in the world go to Japan. Much of it is used to make disposable items such as chopsticks and packing crates.

There is now a much greater understanding of the role that trees play in improving the life of rural communities. Fuelwood can be supplied through techniques such as coppicing, in which a forest is regularly cut back. Certain types of trees can improve the soil by making it more fertile. Crop yields can be increased with the help of

SOIL QUALITY

Although the rainforest is rich in biodiversity, rainforest soil is of poor quality. This is because the recycling of nutrients takes place mainly above the surface in the plants of the rainforest. In temperate forests, nutrient recycling mainly takes place within the soil. So a clear-cut forest in the north often creates good agricultural land—as was the case in Great Britain and the U.S. In the tropics, however, farmers may only be able to use a plot of cleared rainforest land for one or two seasons. Once the nutrients in the soil are used up, the farmer has to cut down more trees for farmland.

Some scientists predict that the construction of highways into the Amazon rainforest, such as the Manaus–Boa Vista Road, will result in the deforestation or damage of 40 percent of Brazil's rainforests.

sheltering trees or shrubs whose root systems prevent soil erosion in open fields.

There is also a greater awareness of the risks from introducing foreign species into an ecosystem. For example, eucalyptus trees are often planted because they are fast growing. But the trees use up so much water they damage the health of other plants.

Unfortunately, it may take too long for subsistence farmers to reap the benefits of slower-growing but more environmentally friendly trees. Small farmers in the developing world lack the financial resources to maintain environmentally friendly forest practices. This forces them to use unsustainable farming methods.

KEY CONCEPTS

Coppicing Coppicing is the cutting back of trees in a forest on a regular basis. This encourages new growth and allows for selective removal of timber. The trees are cut to ground level and allowed to regrow.

Subsistence agriculture
Subsistence agriculture is small-scale farming whereby farmers grow only enough crops to keep their families alive. When a population is large, subsistence agriculture can cause serious deforestation.

The Trans-Amazon Highway
A 3,000-mile (4,840-km) road that runs through Brazil from the Atlantic coast to Peru. The highway has been very important in the development of Brazil's economy. Vast amounts of forest had to be cut down to create the route.

Duties: The reforestation of deforested land
Education: None required
Interests: Physical fitness and the outdoors

Navigate to the tree planter's Web site: www.tree-planter.com for information on related careers. Also click on www.ccohs.ca/youngworkers/treeplanters.html for more information about tree planting jobs.

Careers in Focus

While very few people ever make a career out of tree planting, it is a popular summer job among university and college students, particularly in North America. During the spring and summer, tens of thousands of students head to the mountains and forests to plant hundreds of millions of tree seedlings. Throughout the summer, teams of planters are transported to deforested areas to plant seedling trees. The workers must dig planting holes at predetermined intervals, using a shovel or **dibble**. The workers must then place a seedling in the hole and pack the soil around the plant. Workers typically plant between 1,000 and 2,000 trees per day, depending on the region and their experience. For the duration of the summer, planters work, and often live, outdoors in makeshift campgrounds, logging camps, and bush camps.

While tree planting can be a rewarding job, it also demands a high level of physical fitness. It is a difficult and strenuous job. Tree planters often suffer from back problems, dehydration, heat exhaustion, and **tendinitis**. Other hazards include insect bites and animal encounters. Tree planters are typically paid by the number of trees they plant.

Tree planters sometimes engage in other areas of forestry work, such as attaching choker cables to logs, brush clearing, pesticide spraying, and cleaning logging sites. They usually work for logging companies and contractors.

Hugging the Trees

Most governments have agreed that the world's forests need to be protected. But they have not yet agreed on how to do so. Even the 1992 United Nations' Conference on Environment and Development was unable to agree on a list of forest protection recommendations. Nongovernmental organizations (NGOs) have been the most successful at saving forests.

The World Commission on Forests and Sustainable Development (WCFSD) was set up in 1995 to enable governments to work toward

an international agreement on forest management. The WCFSD has made many recommendations. These include creating a system to judge the **ecological** value of forests, creating ways to use forested land without destroying it, educating people, identifying forest abuses, and rewarding good forest practices.

Despite the lack of a global forest agreement, attitudes toward forests have improved. Most nations now realize that sustainable forest management is necessary. Environmental impact, biodiversity, and the rights of indigenous peoples must also be considered. Certification of wood products has become increasingly popular. Certification lets consumers know that the wood in the products they buy has come from properly managed forests.

The World Bank and the World Wildlife Fund (WWF) have created a "Forest Alliance" to work with governments, companies, and local citizens to reduce deforestation around the world. The alliance has two goals that it aims to achieve by 2005. The first is to add more than 193,000 square miles (500,000 sq km) of newly protected forest and to ensure that another 193,000 square miles (500,000 sq km) of forest is properly managed. The second goal is to certify 772,200 square miles (2 million sq km) of the world's commercially managed forests— half in tropical regions and half in temperate and boreal forest regions.

The Forest Alliance has also established forest conservation programs in certain areas. Examples include Latvia's boreal forests, Mexico's tropical dry

The FAO works closely with governments and local communities to combat the causes and effects of deforestation.

CENTRAL AFRICA UNITES TO PROTECT THE CONGO BASIN

In December 2000, the battle against poaching and illegal logging in the Congo Basin received a significant boost when three central-African nations agreed to share management of a 10,800-square-mile (28,000 sq km) section of rainforest. The Democratic Republic of Congo, the Central African Republic, and Cameroon agreed to create Sangha Park, an area of more than 3,860 square miles (10,000 sq km). The countries are working to harmonize their forestry laws and implement a common management system on anti-poaching measures, ecological monitoring, and logging.

forests, and the rainforests of Papua New Guinea, Liberia, and the Laos–Vietnam border.

The world's two largest conservation NGOs are the WWF and the World Conservation Union (IUCN). These two organizations are working together to develop a strategy to protect the world's forests. Their goal is to create more protected forest areas, to reduce forest damage, to encourage good forest management outside of protected areas, and to promote the use of forest products without damaging the environment.

Protected areas have been created to conserve rare trees such as old-growth giant cedars, sequoias, Douglas fir trees, and giant redwoods (pictured).

The World Resources Institute (WRI) is trying to promote conservation of the remaining natural forests with its "Forest Frontiers" initiative. The WRI's "Global Forest Watch" works with NGOs in different countries to keep track of the condition of forests around the world. In addition, many other NGOs and local groups are working to save the forests. These include the World Rainforest Movement, Conservation International, Friends of the Earth, Greenpeace, and the Rainforest Action Network.

Meanwhile, the forest industry has been influenced by the arguments about forest loss. The Finnish company AssiDomän is the world's largest publicly held forest owner. AssiDomän has accepted

---

Sustainable forest management can only be achieved if supported by local communities.

---

independent certification by the Forest Stewardship Council. MacMillan Bloedel is a Canadian company that has been criticized for clear-cutting old-growth forests in British Columbia. Public pressure has forced the company to reassess its forestry

practices. In total, about 600 companies are enrolled in the Forest Stewardship Council certification program.

The problem of deforestation cannot be solved by NGOs, nor can it be ended by international law. Sustainable forest management can only be achieved if supported by local communities. This means that more fundamental problems have to be tackled. They include addressing issues of poverty, recognizing local land rights, creating a fair and environmentally friendly trading system, providing debt relief for poor countries, and making logging companies responsible for the health of the environment.

KEY CONCEPTS

NGOs NGO stands for nongovernmental organization. NGOs are not part of any political party and are not created for profit. NGOs have become increasingly important in the struggle to protect the world's forests. Examples include the WWF and IUCN.

Protected forests Protected forests are those that are left in their natural state. The government sets certain areas of forest aside as protected areas. This is done to preserve

the biodiversity of a region. Commercial logging is not allowed in protected forests.

Properly managed forests Properly managed forests are commercial forests in which the company makes sure that their forest practices are not damaging forest ecosystems.

Certification Today, only 10 percent of the world's forest area is protected from deforestation by law. Certification of wood products is considered to be one

answer to the problem of forest loss. To be certified, a company has to meet certain standards. In forestry, certification means that wood products have come from timber that was logged legally. Chain-of-custody certification refers to a process in which wood products are tracked all the way from forest to retailer. This encourages sustainable forest management.

CERTIFICATION AND THE FOREST STEWARDSHIP COUNCIL

The Forest Stewardship Council (FSC) was created in 1993 with support from the WWF and other NGOs. The FSC introduced an international system of labeling forest products. Forest products with the FSC logo are certified by independent organizations, such as Smart Wood in the United States or the United Kingdom's Soil Association. FSC certification confirms that wood products have come from forests that meet the following FSC principles:

1. Forest management shall respect all applicable laws of the country in which they occur;

2. Long-term tenure and use rights to the land and forest resources shall be clearly defined and documented;

3. The legal and customary rights of indigenous peoples shall be recognized and respected;

4. The long-term social and economic well-being of forest workers and local communities shall be maintained;

5. Operations shall encourage the efficient use of the forest's multiple products and services to ensure economic viability and a wide range of environmental and social benefits;

6. Forest management shall conserve biological diversity and its associated values, water resources, soils, and unique and fragile ecosystems and landscapes, and, by so doing, maintain the ecological functions and the integrity of the forest;

7. A management plan that is appropriate to the scale and intensity of the operations shall be written, carried out, and kept up to date. The long-term objectives of management, and the means of achieving them, shall be clearly stated;

8. Monitoring—appropriate to the scale and intensity of forest management—shall be conducted to assess the condition of the forest, yields of forest products, chain of custody, management activities, and their social and environmental impacts;

9. Management activities in high conservation value forests shall maintain or enhance the attributes that define such forests;

10. Plantations shall be planned and managed in accordance with these principles; while plantations can provide social and economic benefits, and can contribute to satisfying the world's needs for forest products, they should complement the management of, reduce pressures on, and promote conservation of natural forests.

Duties: Enforcing environmental regulations
Education: A bachelor's degree in environmental management
Interests: Protecting the environment, law enforcement, and public relations

Navigate to the Environmental Careers Web site: www.eco.org for information on related careers. Also click on www.environmental-jobs.com for more information about environmental officer jobs.

Careers in Focus

Environmental officers—sometimes called "green cops"—are trained to investigate violations of environmental regulations. Environmental officers often receive tips from concerned members of the community who report suspicious activity in their neighborhoods, such as illegal dumping or logging. Environmental officers have power similar to that of other law enforcement officers. They may lay charges against companies and individuals who break environmental laws.

Environmental officers also inspect industrial sites to see if they are respecting regulations. Companies are often given a certain period of time to clean up their operations. In extreme cases, an officer has the power to shut down an operation.

Environmental officers working with the Brazilian Environmental Agency (IBAMA) regularly catch and fine companies and individuals running illegal logging operations in the country's rainforests. Unfortunately, a lack of funding and resources means that the IBAMA catches only a fraction of the illegal loggers. Government officials in Brazil estimate that 80 percent of all logging in the Brazilian Amazon is illegal. With more funding and help from NGOs, such as Greenpeace, it is hoped that environmental officers in Brazil will be able to clamp down on illegal logging in the country.

Time Line of Events

About 8,000 years ago
Forests cover about 23 million square miles (60 million sq km) of the planet.

6000 B.C.
Deforestation results in the decline of communities in southern Jordan.

2600 B.C.
Large-scale commercial logging operations are conducted in ancient Lebanon. The lumber is exported to Egypt and Sumeria.

500 B.C.
Greek cities along the coast become **landlocked** as soil fills in the mouths and bays of rivers. The soil is carried down the rivers from deforested land upstream.

427–347 B.C.
Greek philosopher Plato compares the erosion of deforested hills and mountains in Greece to the skeleton of a human body: "All the richer and softer parts have fallen away and the mere skeleton of the land remains."

Around A.D. 1600
The deforestation of Easter Island leads to a decline in the island's population and civilization.

1621
The pilgrims in Massachusetts send a ship called *Fortune* back to England full of timber. The export of timber from the New World has begun.

1862
American Henry David Thoreau calls for the government to set aside protected areas of land for the benefit of future generations.

His ideas on conservation are discussed in his essay "Walking," in which he states, "In wilderness is the preservation of the world."

1872
Yellowstone National Park becomes the world's first national park.

1901
Theodore Roosevelt becomes president of the United States. Forest conservation and preservation are an important part of his domestic policy.

1916
The United States Congress passes legislation that establishes the National Park Service.

1970
Brazilian rainforests remain an untouched natural resource.

1985
More than 77,220 square miles (200,000 sq km) of Brazilian rainforest has been cut or destroyed.

1993
The Forest Stewardship Council (FSC) is founded.

1993
Half of the coastal forests of Clayoquot Sound on Vancouver Island are opened for logging.

1995
The World Commission on Forests and Sustainable Development (WCFSD) is set up.

<hr />

Heavy logging and slash-and-burn agriculture have been blamed for an increase in tropical forest fires.

1996
WWF starts the "Forests for Life" campaign.

1997
According to Greenpeace, international logging companies invest $100 million in the Amazon.

1997–98
El Niño causes drought conditions in normally wet areas of rainforest, where yearlong rainfall usually protects the trees from fires.

1997–98
Fire destroys 7,720 square miles (20,000 sq km) of forest in Brazil and a similar-sized area in Indonesia. Mexico and Central America also experience fires over very large areas.

1998
The United States and Canada experience an ice storm. In the U.S. alone, some 7,720 square miles (20,000 sq km) of forest are severely damaged, causing losses of more than $1 billion.

1999
Greenpeace establishes a permanent base in Manaus, Brazil. They begin conducting investigations into illegal and destructive logging practices in remote areas of the Amazon.

1999
Hundreds of fires rage in Indonesia as large-scale land clearance efforts continue.

2000
The FAO's *Global Forest Resources Assessment 2000*, the most comprehensive survey of forest conditions, is released.

2001
About 347,500 square miles (900,000 sq km), or 2 percent, of global forest is certified under the Forest Stewardship Council.

2001
Greenpeace calls for the government of Brazil to reduce deforestation to zero by 2010.

Concept Web

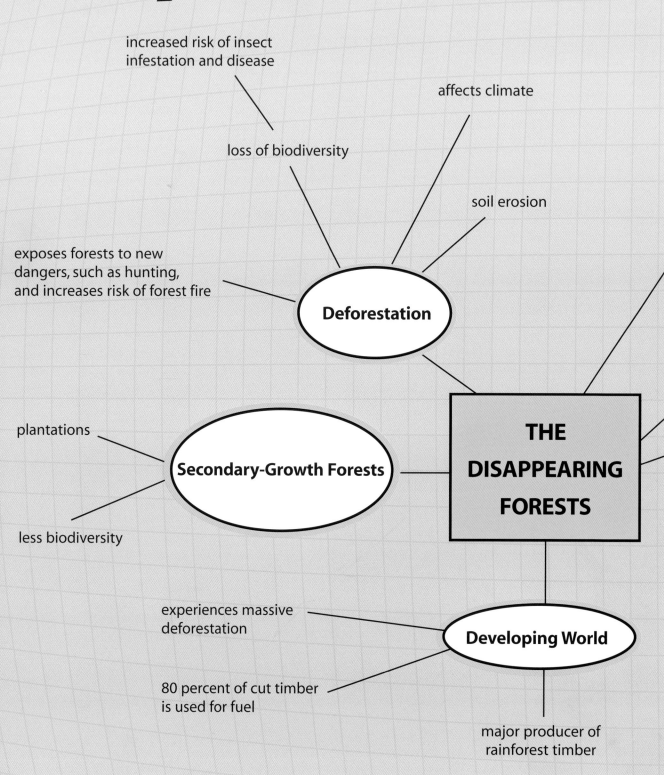

increased risk of insect
infestation and disease

affects climate

loss of biodiversity

soil erosion

exposes forests to new
dangers, such as hunting,
and increases risk of forest fire

Deforestation

plantations

Secondary-Growth Forests

THE DISAPPEARING FORESTS

less biodiversity

experiences massive
deforestation

Developing World

80 percent of cut timber
is used for fuel

major producer of
rainforest timber

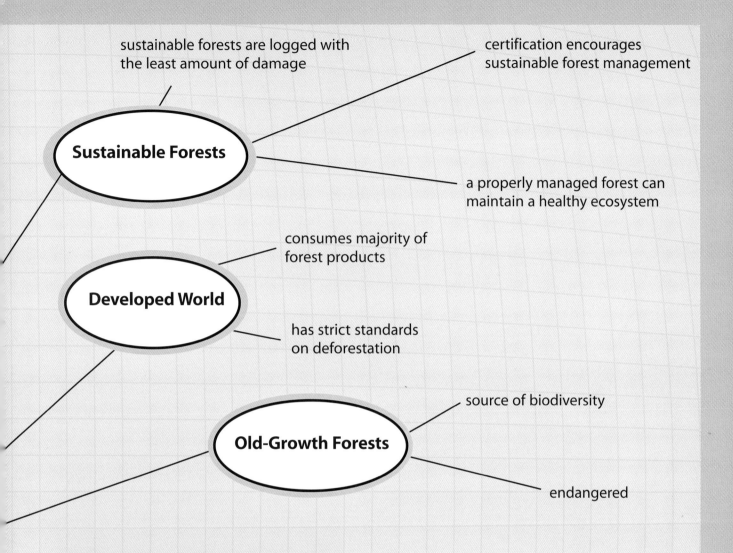

Sustainable Forests

sustainable forests are logged with the least amount of damage

certification encourages sustainable forest management

a properly managed forest can maintain a healthy ecosystem

Developed World

consumes majority of forest products

has strict standards on deforestation

Old-Growth Forests

source of biodiversity

endangered

MAKE YOUR OWN CONCEPT WEB

A concept web is a useful summary tool. It can also be used to plan your research or help you write an essay or report. To make your own concept web, follow the steps below:

- You will need a large piece of unlined paper and a pencil.
- First, read through your source material, such as *The Disappearing Forests* in the Understanding Global Issues series.
- Write the main idea, or concept, in large letters in the center of the page.
- On a sheet of lined paper, jot down all words, phrases, or lists that you know are connected with the concept. Try to do this from memory.
- Look at your list. Can you group your words and phrases in certain topics or themes? Connect the different topics with lines to the center, or to other "branches."
- Critique your concept web. Ask questions about the material on your concept web: Does it all make sense? Are all the links shown? Could there be other ways of looking at it? Is anything missing?
- What more do you need to find out? Develop questions for those areas you are still unsure about or where information is missing. Use these questions as a basis for further research.

Quiz

Multiple Choice

1. Which of the following is not one of the seven biomes found on Earth?
   - a) tundra
   - b) taiga
   - c) mountain
   - d) ocean

2. What percentage of global forest cover is covered by replanted forests?
   - a) 3 percent
   - b) 7 percent
   - c) 15 percent
   - d) 24 percent

3. In which country can the Kailua Forest be found?
   - a) Finland
   - b) Brazil
   - c) Sweden
   - d) New Zealand

4. What percentage of all tropical timber exports in the world go to Japan?
   - a) 13 percent
   - b) 26 percent
   - c) 32 percent
   - d) 40 percent

5. The three main causes of deforestation in Costa Rica are:
   - a) cattle, timber, and banana products
   - b) cattle, timber, and rubber products
   - c) logging, settlement, and soil erosion
   - d) logging, settlement, and road construction

6. The wax palm is:
   - a) the smallest tree in the world
   - b) Colombia's national tree
   - c) the easiest tree to climb
   - d) an important source of rubber

Where Did It Happen?

1. Construction of the 3,000-mile (4,840 km) Trans-Amazon Highway destroys vast amounts of forestland.
2. The creation of Sangha Park establishes a protected area of rainforest, co-managed by three nations.
3. Part of Clayoquot Sound is opened for logging.
4. In 1998, an ice storm damages some 7,720 square miles (20,000 sq km) of forest.
5. Cities become landlocked as soil fills in the bays and mouths of rivers.
6. The construction of railroad tracks results in the loss of millions of trees.
7. The original Caledonian Forest disappears.
8. In mid-1999, hundreds of fires are set in order to clear large areas of land.
9. A 2000 report by the FAO announces that 3.3 million square miles (8.6 million sq km) is the greatest amount of forest found within one country.
10. The world's largest publicly held forest company, AssiDomän, agrees to accept independent certification by the Forest Stewardship Council.

True or False

1. The soil found in the Amazon River basin is ideal for farming.
2. An "open forest" is one in which at least 10 percent of an area is covered by the tree canopy.
3. Satellite images are the best method for gathering information about the world's forest cover.
4. Brazil has the largest amount of the world's forests.
5. Two-thirds of the world's forests are commercial forests.

Answers on page 53

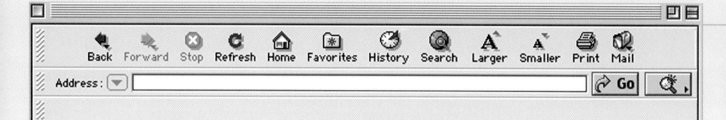

Internet Resources

International organizations and nongovernmental organizations involved in forest conservation:

WWF

http://panda.org

Since it was founded in 1961, WWF has become one of the world's largest and most effective independent organizations dedicated to the conservation of nature. It has reached this status through a consistent record of conservation achievements.

IUCN

http://www.iucn.org

The World Conservation Union was founded in 1948. It brings together 78 states, 112 government agencies, 735 NGOs, 35 affiliates, and some 10,000 scientists and experts from 181 countries in a unique worldwide partnership. Its mission is to influence, encourage, and assist societies throughout the world to conserve the integrity and diversity of nature and to ensure that the use of natural resources is equitable and ecologically sustainable.

FAO

http://www.fao.org

The Food and Agriculture Organization of the United Nations was created in 1945. The FAO works to raise standards of living, increase levels of nutrition, and improve agricultural productivity around the world.

Some Web sites stay current longer than others. To find other forest Web sites, enter terms such as "rainforest," "Amazon," or "logging" into a search engine.

Further Reading

Bonnicksen, Thomas M. *America's Ancient Forests: From the Ice Age to the Age of Discovery*. New York: John Wiley & Sons, 2000.

Küchli, Christian. *Forests of Hope: Stories of Regeneration*. Gabriola Island, British Columbia: New Society Publishers, 1997.

May, Elizabeth, and Farley Mowat. *At the Cutting Edge: The Crisis in Canada's Forests*. San Francisco: Sierra Club Books, 1998.

Rosenblatt, Naomi. *Rainforests for Beginners*. Environmental Studies Series. New York: Writers and Readers Publishing, 1992.

Rowh, Mark, and Christopher M. Wille. *Opportunities in Forestry Careers*. Vgm Opportunities Series. Columbus: McGraw Hill–NTC, 1998.

Royte, Elizabeth. *The Tapir's Morning Bath: Mysteries of the Tropical Rain Forest and the Scientists Who Are Trying to Solve Them*. Boston: Houghton Mifflin Company, 2001.

Answers

Multiple Choice
1. c)   2. a)   3. a)   4. d)   5. a)   6. b)

Where Did It Happen?
1. Brazil   2. Congo Basin   3. Vancouver Island   4. New England, southern Ontario, and Quebec   5. Greece   6. India   7. Scotland   8. Indonesia   9. Russia   10. Finland

True or False
1. F   2. T   3. F   4. F   5. T

Glossary

boreal: relating to the northern forested areas of the North Temperate Zone

botany: the science of plants

capitalism: an economic system in which the production and distribution of wealth is controlled mainly by individuals and corporations

cash crops: crops that are considered easy to sell, such as bananas

charcoal: a type of fuel made from wood

commercial: capable of producing a profit

dibble: a small handheld device used to make holes in the ground

ecological: the relationship between organisms and their environment

environmentalists: people who are interested in protecting the environment

erosion: the removal of the top layer of soil by natural forces, such as water, glaciers, or wind

eucalyptus: tall, fast-growing trees native to Australia

horticulture: the science of cultivating plants

indigenous: native to a region

landlocked: surrounded by land, without access to the ocean

lignin: a compound that hardens and strengthens the cell walls in plants

multinational: a company with operations in two or more countries

plantations: large farms used to raise crops

railroad ties: wooden beams used at intervals to support railroad tracks

sub-tropical: the region that lies between the tropical and temperate zones

tannin: a plant product used in tanning animal skins to make leather; also used to make dyes and inks

temperate: related to the geographic zones that lie between the tropics and the polar circles

tendinitis: inflammation of a tendon

topsoil: the fertile upper layer of soil

transpiration: the evaporation of water from plant cells

tree canopy: upper layer of vegetation in a forest, which creates a type of ceiling

tropical: from the tropics, the region between the Tropic of Cancer and the Tropic of Capricorn

Index

Photo Credits

Cover: Trucks Carrying Logs on Sabah's Main Logging Track Close to the Kalimantan Border, Borneo (**DigitalVision**); **Title page**: **DigitalVision**; **Corel**: pages 8, 16, 32b, 44; **DigitalVision**: pages 19, 33, 47; **Victor Englebert**: pages 2/3, 6, 7, 20, 22, 30, 34, 38; **FAO photo/R. Faidutt**: page 36; **FAO photo/ F. McDougall**: page 40; **Mike Grandmaison**: pages 9, 14, 25, 37, 42; **Kindra Clineff Photography**: pages 13, 15; **Thomas Kitchin/Tom Stack & Associates**: page 39; **PhotoDisc**: page 32t; **Catherine Rimmi**: page 45; **Rob & Ann Simpson/Photo Agora**: page 4; **U.S. Geological Survey, EROS Data Center**: pages 10, 11, 35; **Wellcome Trust Medical Photographic Library**: page 21.